I LOVE HAMSTERS

by Harold T. Rober

BUMBA BOOKS™

LERNER PUBLICATIONS ◆ MINNEAPOLIS

Note to Educators:

Throughout this book, you'll find critical thinking questions. These can be used to engage young readers in thinking critically about the topic and in using the text and photos to do so.

Lerner Publications Company
A division of Lerner Publishing Group, Inc.
241 First Avenue North
Minneapolis, MN 55401 USA

For reading levels and more information, look up this title at www.lernerbooks.com.

Library of Congress Cataloging-in-Publication Data

The Cataloging-in-Publication Data for *I Love Hamsters* is on file at the Library of Congress.
ISBN 978-1-5124-1417-2 (lib. bdg.)
ISBN 978-1-5124-1525-4 (pbk.)
ISBN 978-1-5124-1526-1 (EB pdf)

Manufactured in the United States of America
1 — VP — 7/15/16

LERNER
e
SOURCE

Expand learning beyond the printed book. Download free, complementary educational resources for this book from our website, www.lerneresource.com.

Table of Contents

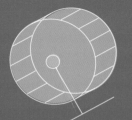

Pet Hamsters

A hamster is a small pet.

It fits in my hands.

A hamster needs a cage.

A hamster should live alone.

Why does a pet hamster need a cage?

We put wood chips

in the cage.

Our hamster builds a nest

with the wood chips.

We clean the cage outside.

We will put in new wood chips.

Why should you keep a hamster's cage clean?

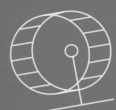

We give our hamster a piece of wood.

It chews the wood.

This keeps its teeth short.

Why do you think wood is good for hamsters to chew on?

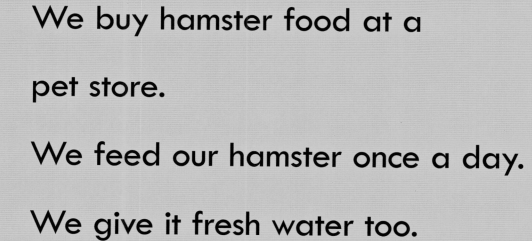

We buy hamster food at a
pet store.

We feed our hamster once a day.

We give it fresh water too.

Hamsters like to run.

Our hamster runs

on a wheel.

It runs through a tube.

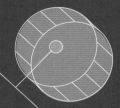

Hamsters sleep during the day.
They are awake and make noise
at night.
We do not keep the cage
in a bedroom.

19

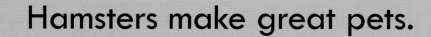

Hamsters make great pets.

They can live for three years.

Hamster Supplies

wheel

tube

cage

water

wood chips

food

Picture Glossary

cage

a container in which
a pet is kept

nest

a place built by animals
to live in or have babies

tube

a hollow object
hamsters run through

**wood
chips**

small and thin
pieces of wood

Index

Read More

Graubart, Norman. *My Hamster.* New York: PowerKids Press, 2014.

Meister, Cari. *Hamsters.* Minneapolis: Bullfrog Books, 2015.

Murray, Julie. *Hamsters.* Minneapolis: Abdo Kids, 2016.

Photo Credits

The images in this book are used with the permission of: © kmrep/iStock.com, p. 5; © AlexKalashnikov/Shutterstock.com, pp. 6, 23 (top left); © Kerstin Waurick/iStock.com, pp. 8–9, 23 (top right); © 2xSamara.com/Shutterstock.com, p. 10; © Leonid Eremeychuk/Shutterstock.com, p. 13; © spectrelabs/iStock.com, p. 14; © Khmel/iStock.com, pp. 16–17; © Punyaphat Larpsomboon/Shutterstock.com, pp. 18, 23 (bottom right); © Stellajune3700/iStock.com, p. 21; © Natalia Yudenich/Shutterstock.com, p. 22 (bottom left); © Watcha/iStock.com, p. 22 (bottom right); © Hurst Photo/Shutterstock.com, p. 22 (top right); © Beth Van Trees/Shutterstock.com, p. 22 (top left); © AlexKalashnikov/iStock.com, p. 23 (bottom left).

Front Cover: © Victoria Rak/Shutterstock.com.